C000174112

GERMAN
NAVAL
AIR SERVICE
Alex Imrie

Front cover illustration:
Brandenburg W29 2532 was
from a 30-aircraft production
batch ordered in April 1918.
Powered by a 150hp Benz
engine and fitted with two
forward-firing machine-guns, it
was accepted by the Navy in late
July and is shown wearing the
double white bands on the rear
fuselage that denoted the
Starboard Watch of Norderney
Naval Air Station.

Back cover illustrations: see
plates 17, 26 and 89.

1. Brandenburg W 477, its 160hp Mercedes engine running, is lifted off its railway car by crane and swung out to clear the Zeebrugge Mole prior to being lowered into the water. The observer, who was responsible for the correctness of the lifting shackle, is standing on the edge of his cockpit ready to release the crane's hook when lowering is complete. The Rating (extreme right) walking away with the tail line prevents the aircraft from turning out of wind while suspended from the crane. Containers for fuel, oil and water can be seen on the railway car. (See also photo No. 30)

GERMAN NAVAL AIR SERVICE

Alex Imrie

ARMS AND
ARMOUR

▲2

2. Friedrichshafen FF33L 1010 being retrieved from the Baltic following an accident on the bombing range of the observers'

▼3

school at Wiek on the island of Rügen, summer 1918. Powered by a 150hp Benz engine, this aircraft had an unrestricted

front-line designation and was known as a CHFT type, meaning that it was equipped with a movable gun for the observer

and was fitted with wireless-telegraphy transmitting and receiving equipment.

3. From March 1912 it was laid down that all German naval aeroplanes had to be of amphibian configuration, a difficult requirement to meet with the marginal engine power then available. By discarding the wheels fitted to the central Coulmann float of the Albatros WD3 (70hp Mercedes), *Oberleutnant zur See* Langfeld was able to make the first water take-off on 5 July 1912. When the wheels were fitted again, a system was used that enabled them to be raised clear of the water. To reduce water resistance further and allow acceleration to flying speed, the wing tip floats could also be raised by means of the large handwheel on the port side of the nacelle.

INTRODUCTION

First published in Great Britain in 1989 by Arms and Armour Press, Artillery House, Artillery Row, London SW1P 1RT.

Distributed in the USA by Sterling Publishing Co. Inc., 2 Park Avenue, New York, NY 10016.

Distributed in Australia by Capricorn Link (Australia) Pty. Ltd., P.O. Box 665, Lane Cove, New South Wales 2066, Australia.

© Arms and Armour Press Limited, 1989
All rights reserved. No part of this book may be reproduced or transmitted in any form or by any means electronic or mechanical including photocopying recording or any information storage and retrieval system without permission in writing from the Publisher.

British Library Cataloguing in Publication Data:
Imrie, Alex
German naval air service. –
(Vintage aviation fotofax)
1. German air forces, to 1985
I. Title   II. Series
358.4′00943
ISBN 0-85368-920-2

Designed and edited by DAG Publications Ltd.
Designed by David Gibbons; layout by Cilla Eurich; typeset by Ronset Typesetters Ltd, Darwen, Lancashire, and Typesetters (Birmingham) Ltd, Warley, West Midlands; camerawork by M&E Reproductions, North Fambridge, Essex; printed and bound in Great Britain by The Alden Press, Oxford.

The German Naval Air Service entered the war completely unprepared: only six seaplanes were available to the North Sea area while three machines were allocated to the Baltic. The number of trained personnel stood at 20 officer pilots, there were no trained air observers at all, and while some pilots also flew as observer, often mechanics were taken aloft for this purpose. Only one airship (L3) was on charge, which due to the short range of the seaplanes and their lack of wireless was seen as the more reliable reconnaissance vehicle, and steps were afoot to bring more airships rapidly into commission. Pre-war thinking decreed that the British Fleet would impose a close blockade on the German coast and the German Fleet would consequently be forced to fight a decisive action close to its bases. Because of this, the naval air strength was deployed entirely for the protection of the German Bight and the observation of the entrance to the Baltic Sea.

It is not possible in a book of this nature to tell the whole fascinating story of how this nucleus grew into the efficient naval air arm that existed in November 1918, but the material used here has been selected to show important aspects of the application of the airship and the aeroplane in naval service, and to give an insight into the rapid development that took place in the few years of the force's existence. It should be remembered that although attention tends to be focused on the excitement of aerial fighting, bombing attacks and other encounters with enemy forces, the major part of the operational work comprised many thousands of monotonous flying hours on reconnaissance duties, where the whole sea areas within the radius of action of the aircraft were kept under constant surveillance and charted to a very high degree of accuracy – thus truly fulfilling the role envisaged for Germany's *Marineflieger* from the beginning.

By the end of the war a total of 16,122 officers, NCOs and men comprised the strength of the heavier-than-air force, of whom 2,116 were employed on flying duties. Some 1,500 aircraft were on charge, of which over half were front-line machines, approximately one quarter of that number being landplanes. Some 6,000 officers, NCOs and men and sixteen airships marked the strength of the *Marine-Luftschiff-Abteilung*, and this formation, equipped during the period of hostilities with 64 airships, had been responsible for carrying out 1,148 reconnaissance and 200 bombing sorties against the United Kingdom, Russia and Italy. The organization encompassed 32 naval air stations and seventeen land aerodromes within the areas of the North Sea, Flanders, Baltic and Kurland, Black Sea, Mediterranean, Adriatic coast and Germany itself. Following the demobilization of the German Naval Air Service in 1919–20, that service never again appeared as a separate air arm, naval aviation being an integral part of the *Luftwaffe* during the 1933–1945 period and of the *Bundeswehr* up to the present time.

My interest in World War One aviation started when I read both fact and fiction in magazines like *Popular Flying* and *Flying Aces* during the 1930s and received an enormous impetus when, after World War Two, as an airline pilot, I was based in West Berlin for 15 years and was able personally to meet many of the aviators about whom I had previously only read. I was invited to attend the informal monthly meetings of the *Kameradschaftliche Vereinigung der Marineflieger* (KMF) and in this naval fliers old comrades' association I was able to enhance my knowledge of World War One German naval aviation, being eventually elected into the KMF as a special member. This was a very great honour, and I am intensely proud of this relationship that allows me to wear the golden-winged anchor insignia of the KMF.

Most of the photographs presented here have originated either from individual ex-marine aviators or the KMF-*Bildsammlung*. Special thanks must be made to *Kapitän zur See* Hermann Lessing, *Flugzeug-Oberstabsingenieur* Franz Wangemann, *Major Doktor* Hans Boetticher and to other members of the KMF, as well as Peter M. Grosz and Bengt Wahlström for their constant interest and provision of information.

Alex Imrie

▼4

4. Official dissatisfaction with the slow progress of the marine aeroplane led to the first German Seaplane Competition, held at Heiligendamm in August-September 1912. Various manufacturers submitted what were basically landplanes fitted with floats, and although only two (Aviatik and Albatros) met the requirements, the official view was that the problems of amphibian operation had been solved. In a further internal selection, the RMA *(Reichs Marine Amt –* German Admiralty) purchased this Albatros (80hp Argus) entry from funds raised by the West Prussian section of the *Deutscher-Luftflotten-Verein.*

▼5

Flugplatz Johannisthal.

5. The airship was judged suitable for combatting submarines and mines, undertaking reconnaissance and capable of carrying out bombing raids on enemy shore installations. In the 1911 Naval Estimates the purchase of one airship was permitted. Ordered in April 1912, the first naval airship (L1, shown here) was ferried from Friedrichshafen via Emden and Kiel to Johannisthal in October 1912. It performed valuable reconnaissance service during the 1913 Autumn Fleet manoeuvres but was destroyed near Heligoland by a storm on 9 September with the loss of 14 members of its crew. However, on that day the second naval airship (L2) made its maiden flight; it was ferried to Johannisthal eleven days later.

6▲   7▼

8 ▼

6. In order to evaluate current foreign marine aircraft techniques several machines were bought from other countries, including an Avro 503 seaplane from Britain. Following acceptance tests, the Avro was flown to Heligoland for the Autumn Fleet manoeuvres by Langfeld, carrying a passenger, in September 1913. This was the first flight by a seaplane from the German mainland to Heligoland. Four seaplanes were deployed in the manoeuvres, but three of them were considered unsuitable for operational use; the Avro, however, generally gave excellent results.

7. Putzig, near Danzig, was selected as the site for the German naval *Flugversuchstation* (Flight Experimental Station) since it possessed a wide flat area of grassland, providing a natural land aerodrome, and a coastal area protected from rough wave conditions by the Hela peninsula, giving an excellent seaplane harbour – thus meeting both of the requirements for the operation of amphibious aircraft. The machines seen here in 1913 are the Albatros monplane, designed by Ernst Heinkel and flown with success by Helmuth Hirth in the Bodensee Competition, and the Avro (D12) bought from Britain.

8. Seaplanes were allocated consecutive numbers which at first were prefixed with 'D' for *Doppeldecker* (biplane) or 'E' for *Eindecker* (monoplane); however, after number 20 had been issued, the use of the prefix was discontinued. Shown here is Ago pusher seaplane D15 at Kolberg on 12 February 1914; built in 1913, this machine was powered by an 80hp Argus engine. The marine number marked on the nacelle is also carried on the outer surfaces of the outboard rudders. Following mobilization, 'Kiel' was additionally marked on the outboard sides of the floats.

9. Curtiss flying-boat D18 approaching the slipway at Kiel-Holtenau. Continued evaluation of the flying-boat type of marine aircraft resulted in the RMA ordering examples from Albatros, Oertz and Friedrichshafen, as well as continuing to purchase foreign flying-boats, including a Sopwith Bat-Boat powered by a 200hp Canton-Unne. However, this configuration never really found favour for operational use.

▲9　▼10

10. Although flying-boats continued to be evaluated, the Germans considered the twin-float seaplane to possess better seaworthiness, especially in the rough wave conditions that exist in the North Sea. It was the reliable performance of the Avro 503 that confirmed this thinking and the RMA asked several manufacturers to produce seaplanes based on the Avro concept. This is the Ago which used the same engine as the Avro (100hp Gnome), ten machines being ordered in February 1914 in the first series order by the RMA.

▼11

11. Albatros GmbH of Johannisthal were awarded a five-aircraft order, their Avro version being powered by either the 100hp Argus or Mercedes six-cylinder water-cooled engine. Three machines were to be fitted with wireless receiving equipment, and the weight of this plus the necessary 6 metres high aerial mast seen here, had to be carried during the acceptance trials. The contract stipulated that the machine's performance had to equal that of the Avro and that the two aircraft without wireless equipment were to be fitted with dual flying controls.

12. Friedrichshafen FF19 seaplanes 25 and 26 enjoying unusually calm sea conditions in the Heligoland Bight. They were part of a five-aircraft order placed in February 1914, harbingers of the three-bay Friedrichshafen seaplane layout that became the FF33 when powered by the 150hp Benz and the FF49 when the 200hp Benz was used. This basic design, developed over the following two years, had not been improved upon for general workaday duties by the time of the Armistice, and the later models were the most widely used reconnaissance seaplanes in service.

13. Albatros seaplane on the Müggelsee near Berlin. Training new pilots to fly seaplanes was undertaken at Putzig Naval Air Station in West Prussia from October 1914, but eventually the bulk of initial water flying was done in special training sections of the operational air stations, since it was found that it was easier for pupils to appreciate the practical requirements of front-line seaplane handling and thus convert more readily to the operational types of seaplane in a front-line air station environment.

12▲   13▼

14▼

14. Mobilization seaplanes on the ramp at Kiel-Holtenau in August 1914. Aircraft identified in this early wartime photograph include: Rumpler 4BII (150hp Benz) from Warnemünde, Sopwith Bat-Boat 44 (which was never used operationally but merely for short local flights), Friedrichshafen FF19 23 and Albatros B I on floats, which was another machine taken over on the outbreak of war at Warnemünde. All aircraft are carrying red streamers from the bottom wings near the tips for identification purposes and are marked with the Iron Cross type of national insignia.

▲15 ▼16

15. Basic flying training was initially given at schools run by the aircraft manufacturers. Here, in November 1914, a class of naval *ab initio* pilots at Gotha Waggonfabrik's aerodrome pose with their Taube. They are wearing $^3/_4$-length coats, trousers and leggings made of leather, which despite lack of lining were all surprisingly warm, being windproof. Gloves, padded crash helmets with goggles and long woollen scarves complete the official issue of flying clothing assigned to the trainee aviators.

16. Tarmac scene at Johannisthal in early 1915 – NFW and LVG training aircraft used by the FMF (*Freiwilliges Marinefliegerkorps* – Volunteer Naval Flying Corps) in front of the airship sheds. Almost all flying instruction concentrated on the take-off and landing phases of flight. Flying tests consisted of successfully carrying out a number of 'figure-of-eights' flown at an altitude of 200 metres and landings made within a given distance from a specified point on the aerodrome. The nose of the airship 'Hansa', seen in the far building, has been marked with the German national insignia on its undersurfaces.

17. *Korvettenkapitän* Goltz, *Kommandeur* of the FMF, with one of his Albatros B I school machines at Johannisthal. In August 1914 the RMA actioned the pre-war-conceived FMF plan for handling the large number of direct entrants from civilian life required to provide sufficient personnel suitable for training in the trades of pilot, observer and mechanic for both landplane and seaplane units. The FMF was absorbed into the *Marine-Landflieger-Abteilung* in October 1915, which formation was then responsible for the supply of personnel to all naval landplane formations.

18. Following the occupation of the Belgian coast, a seaplane base was established at Zeebrugge in December 1914. Aircraft were kept in the railway station hall at the end of the Mole, fully assembled on specially constructed flat railway cars which carried tools, fabric, dope, etc for minor repairs, as well as supplies of water, fuel and oil. Locomotives were kept with steam up and were always available to pull the trains out on to the Mole and up to the cranes used to lift and lower the seaplanes to the water. In this early 1915 scene no national insignia are displayed on the upper wing surfaces of these Friedrichshafen FF29 seaplanes or the Oertz flying-boat numbered 46, but wing undersurfaces were marked spanwise with the straight-sided cross, as seen on the Oertz's rudder.

17▲ 18▼

19. This Blériot monoplane landing on the Zeebrugge Mole was captured from the Belgian forces during the German advance in Flanders. It was allocated the official naval landplane serial number S 96 and was in continuous use until autumn 1915, when its 80hp Gnome rotary engine was 're-directed' to power one of the new Fokker E monoplanes, engines for which were in short supply.

20. Since the first naval landplanes were training machines, or *Schulflugzeuge*, they were allocated consecutive serial numbers prefixed by the letter 'S'. This system was continued on all naval landplanes, which naturally included front-line machines, until October 1915 when all naval landplanes were given the more appropriate prefix of the letters 'LF', meaning *Land Flugzeug*. This is an Ago C I

▼20 ▲19

21▲

22▲ 23▼

pusher twin-boom biplane seen at Johannisthal before the prefix change.

21. To extend the radius of action of his four-seaplane element and be able to reconnoitre the area north of Libau, the *Kommandeur* of the Putzig Naval Air Station, *Oberleutnant zur See* von Gorrissen, thought of loading his equipment on a ship, thus creating a completely mobile air station. A suitable vessel was available, the 2,425brt British collier *Glyndwr*, which, being without wireless equipment, was not able to receive news of the deteriorating international situation, and had been impounded after docking at Danzig at the beginning of the war. She was converted to a seaplane-carrier in the short space of seven days and gave valuable service in this capacity.

22. *Leutnant zur See* Killinger, who as a Midshipman was observer on Rumpler seaplane 'Kiel 51' operating in the eastern Baltic from SMS *Glyndwr* on 6 April 1915 when, during the bombing of military installations at Libau, his machine was hit by Russian anti-aircraft fire and forced to land. Made a prisoner-of-war, he escaped from Siberia and returned to Germany via Shanghai, Japan, the United States and Norway, arriving at Warnemünde on 6 March 1916. During World War Two Killinger was *Kommandant* of the centre at Oberürsel near Frankfurt where captured Allied aircrew were interrogated.

23. Despite the inscription on this contemporary postcard and the use of a Rumpler rudder, 'Kiel 55' was an early Albatros seaplane, and is shown being towed after retrieval in the Baltic. The crew have carried out the laid-down survival drill well. They have chopped off the outer wing panels to prevent them becoming waterlogged, thus reducing the risk of capsizing; and to 'lighten ship', heavy components from the engine have been detached and dumped overboard. This procedure enabled twin-float seaplanes to remain afloat for long periods in sea conditions well in excess of their seaworthiness rating. Many crews were saved as a result.

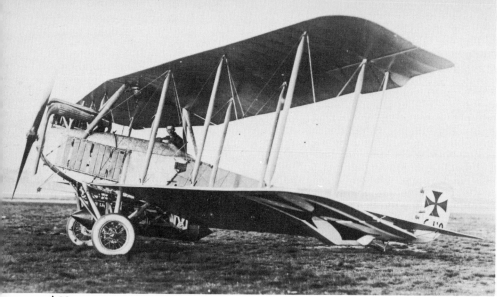

▲24

24. This LVG D4 biplane (later designated S110), powered by a 150hp Benz, had its wing area increased by the insertion of an extra bay and, having a split axle undercarriage and heavy-duty tyres, was used by *Kapitän* Friedländer early in 1915 to investigate the art of dropping a missile of torpedo weight. Sheet lead nailed to the wooden dummy, seen here in its rack under the fuselage, increased its weight on successive experiments, as a result of which Friedländer was able to make the first torpedo drop over

▼25

water at Travemünde on 11 June 1915. In September two torpedoes were dropped that ran true through the water, proving that this type of torpedo release was capable of operational use.

25. When HMS *Maori*, engaged in sketching salient features on the Belgian coast, hit a mine off Blankenberghe and sunk on 7 May 1915, her yard-arm and this flag remained above the water. Despite rough seas, *Oberleutnant zur See* Drekmann (right) landed his

Friedrichshafen FF29 209. Then, with his observer, *Fähnrich zur See* von Blücher, hanging on to the starboard front interplane strut with an open clasp knife held in his teeth, pirate fashion, Drekmann managed after several attempts to position von Blücher so that he could cut the flag free. A hazardous take-off followed and the plucky fliers brought their booty back to Zeebrugge. (British destroyers at sea flew either the Red Ensign or the Union Flag from their yard-arms for recognition purposes,

but the Germans did not know this and were puzzled as to why a Royal Navy vessel should be flying the 'Red Duster'!)

26. *Vizeflugmeister* Kirmss with Albatros B I S77 of *I Marine-Landflieger-Abteilung* at Morseele aerodrome, May 1915. Naval air observers (land or sea) did not have to hold commissioned rank, as was required in the Army Air Service. The weapon is a 25-shot Mauser *Selbstladegewehr* (semi-automatic rifle) and its effectiveness, used from the front cockpit, restricted by bracing wires, struts and the rotating wooden propeller, could not have been great; yet this comprised the only armament for the majority of naval two-seat landplanes until August 1915, when examples of the Albatros C I, armed with a machine-gun on a rotatable ring on the rear observer's cockpit, began to arrive.

27. Naval aircrew members wore flying badges similar to those of their Army colleagues. The naval badges, in silver until mid-1916, then bronze, were finished in gilt and used an eagle in flight motive over Heligoland (left) for seaplane pilots, which was introduced on 31 May 1913; and (right) over a coastal landscape for landplane pilots from 23 February 1915. The air observer's badge in the centre, issued from 28 May 1915, did not differentiate between land and water, and showed a sea eagle perched on a rock looking out to sea. The successful completion of training courses did not automatically bestow the right on the contenders to wear these badges – certain operational experience was also required, and the nature of this varied during the period of hostilities.

27▲

28. The airship operation on the night of 9/10 August 1915 was to have been a squadron attack against London. L12 under *Oberleutnant* Peterson dropped most of its bombs into the sea off Dover, thinking that targets in Harwich and Felixstowe were being attacked. The loss of hydrogen caused by anti-aircraft fire eventually forced L12 to ditch in the English Channel. She was successfully towed into Ostend harbour, but during dismantling the main components of the airship were completely destroyed by an explosion and the resultant fire.

26▲

28▼

29. Early in the morning of 12 August 1915 Flight-Lieutenant Levy in Sopwith Schneider 3717 left Felixstowe on a patrol to the North Hinder lightship. Apparently on his own initiative, he flew on to Zeebrugge where he dropped his bombs on the Mole but was brought down by the carrier pigeon loft attendant whose accurate fire hit the Schneider's petrol tank, causing the engine to stop. Although making a successful forced landing on the water, Levy was unable to get the engine going, so he kicked the floats in, sinking his seaplane before being captured. The Schneider was salvaged, however, completely rebuilt and flown at Zeebrugge. It ended its days in the DELKA travelling exhibition of captured Allied aircraft.

30. Brandenburg W 477 moving away from Zeebrugge Mole after having been lowered by crane to the water. Depending on the wind speed and direction, sometimes full deflection of the control surfaces was needed in

▲ 29   ▼ 30

order to 'sail' the seaplane in the desired direction, especially if taxiing downwind, as here. This machine was based at Zeebrugge from September 1915 and took part in several bombing raids against the United Kingdom, usually crewed by *Leutnants* Rolshoven (pilot) and von Frankenburg (observer).

31. Since the Navy had no facilities of its own for training single-seat pilots, when Fokker E monoplanes were introduced into naval landplane units, naval pilots were sent to the single-seater School attached to *Kampfeinsitzerstaffel I* (*Kest I*) on Sonthofen aerodrome near Mannheim. The first pilot to undertake this conversion course was *Flugmaat* Boedicker, seen (left) with his Army instructor and Fokker E15/15 at Mannheim. Boedicker returned to *II Marine-Feldflieger-Abteilung* at Neumunster in December 1915 and flew the first Fokker E allocated to the *Marine Korps*.

32. Friedrichshafen FF33E 501 at Travemünde during the winter of 1915/16. The machine has been cleared for flight, indicated by the '*Flugbereit*' notice displayed between the floats. Although when delivered this aircraft was a bombing machine, wireless telegraphy appears to have been fitted retrospectively; the windmill-driven generator can be seen fitted to the side of the fuselage near the observer's cockpit.

31▲   32▼

34. Only one Gotha Ursinus seaplane was used by the Navy, being allocated number 120. It is shown on 19 March 1916 on one of its operational flights, when in company with five other seaplanes from Zeebrugge it dropped bombs on Dover, Deal, Ramsgate and Margate, causing 14 fatalities among the civilian population.

35. Airship L20 under *Kapitänleutnant* Stabbert was one of eight detailed to attack targets in the Firth of Forth area on 2 May 1916. Due to strong tailwinds, the bulk of the force abandoned its primary targets. Stabbart, however, kept on his original course but his first navigational pinpoint showed him to be over Loch Ness in the Scottish Highlands. He immediately turned about but knew that battling against the wind he could not reach Germany with his available fuel. The following midday, after almost 22 hours in the air, L20 was ditched on the Norwegian coast, where some of the crew were treated as shipwrecked mariners and returned to Germany.

36. *Fähnrich zur See* Gottard Sachsenberg (centre, seated), an observer with *I Marine-Feldflieger-Abteilung*, found time when running this observers' training course to learn to fly, and was able to return to the Front via the single-seater school at Mannheim as a Fokker pilot. He later led the five *Jagdstaffeln* of the *Marinefeldjagdgeschwader*, achieved 31 victories and was awarded the *Ordre Pour le Mérite* on 5 August 1918. In 1919 he commanded an aircraft formation engaged in the defence of Germany's eastern borders.

▲ 33

33. Two-seater crew of an LVG C I of *II Marine Feldflieger-Abteilung* at Mariakerke in Flanders. The observer at right with the 25cm hand-held camera is *Leutnant* Theo Osterkamp, who later became one of the top-scoring naval fighter piilots; he was credited with 31 victories and was awarded Germany's highest military decoration, the *Ordre Pour le Mérite* on 2 September 1918.

▼ 34

▲37   ▼38

37. The land-based *Riesenflugzeug* (Giant Aeroplane) was evaluated as a possible addition to the naval airship for bombing and long-range scouting purposes. However, experience with RML1 (Reichs Navy Landplane 1) was plagued with difficulties. Engine troubles and structural failures of undercarriage assemblies were eventually overcome and the aircraft participated in some bombing operations on the Eastern Front, until, on a fully loaded night take-off late in August 1916, a double engine failure resulted in this crash into a Russian forest.

38. By mid-1916 the need for single-seat seaplane fighters of good performance caused orders to be placed with various manufacturers for prototype aircraft to be powered by either the Benz or Mercedes six-cylinder engines of 150hp. The first aircraft to be delivered to the seaplane experimental and acceptance centre at Warnemünde (SVK and SAK) was the Rumpler 6BI numbered 751 at the end of August. Following acceptance, it was sent to Zeebrugge where it is seen on its railway car with *Leutnant* Bücker in the cockpit.

39. Tail-end Charlie in 1916! The rear gunner at his station in the stern below the top rudder of L33 illustrates the enormous size of the large Zeppelin rigid airships. L33, under *Kapitänleutnant* Böcker, was brought down by anti-aircraft fire on her first operational flight against Britain on 24 September 1916. L32 was also lost on this raid (*Oberleutnant zur See* Peterson), these two airships being the most up-to-date Zeppelins then in service. Even more serious than the loss of the airships was the loss of the very experienced and capable airship commanders and their crews.

39▲

40. Skeleton of L33 at Little Wigborough after it had been set on fire by its crew; loss of hydrogen due to hits by anti-aircraft gunfire had forced the airship to land in Essex during the early morning of 24 September 1916. The crew under *Kapitänleutnant* Böcker attempted to march to the East Coast, hoping to seize a boat with which to continue their escape, but the 21 Germans were soon captured.

40▼

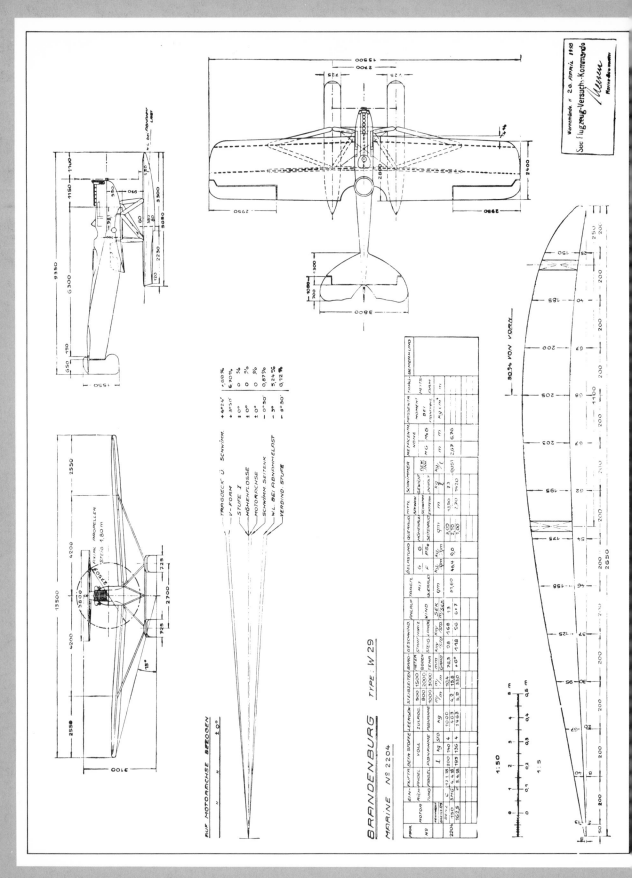

BRANDENBURG TYPE: W 29

MARINE № 2204

GERMAN NAVAL AIR SERVICE

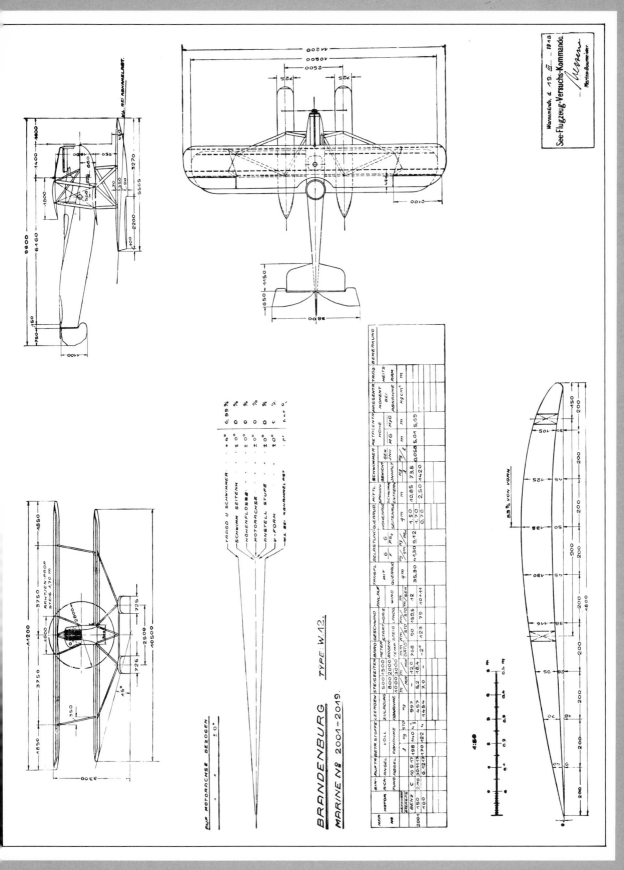

BRANDENBURG   TYPE W.12.

MARINE No 2001÷2019.

EXPLANATORY NOTES

Aircraft procurement for the German Navy was initiated by the RMA (*Reichs Marine Amt* – German Admiralty) placing orders with aircraft manufacturing companies that were experienced in marine aircraft design and construction. The first example of any new type was, when completed, sent to the *See-Flugzeug-Versuchs-Kommando* (SVK = Seaplane Experimental and Testing Command) at Warnemünde for evaluation of its structure, engine systems, and the installation of special equipment, such as armament and wireless, etc. It was during this period that the machine was accurately measured and drawn-up in the form that is given for the types shown in the centre pages of this book, and included rigging details and co-ordinates of aerofoil sections. This action was necessary since the development of certain designs meant that the actual machine delivered could differ from the original manufacturer's drawings that had already been submitted to the SVK. This section of the SVK, under *Marine Baumeister* (Naval Architect) Neesen, also treated significant types of captured enemy aircraft in the same way and the drawings were published in book form in the secret *Atlas Deutscher und Ausländischer Seeflugzeuge* (Atlas of German and Foreign Marine Aircraft), which understandably had a very restricted circulation.

Seaplanes were built to the standards laid down in the *Allgemein Baubestimmungen für Seeflugzeuge der Reichsmarine* (General Construction Regulations for Marine Aircraft of the German Navy) and came to Warnemünde with current national insignia displays and correctly applied individual Marine aircraft numbers. Before being accepted for Naval service, the aircraft were tested for seaworthiness* and flying performance; faults found had obviously to be rectified before the *See-Flugzeug-Abnahme-Kommission* (SAK – Seaplane Acceptance Commission) was satisfied. In addition manufacturers had to institute the changes or modifications found necessary in series aircraft of the same type before sending them to Warnemünde.

Quite significant changes took place during the production span of the main types of seaplanes, not only those caused by different armament, engine and radiator installations, but the arrangement of flying surfaces could vary in shape and outline. When this variance became too profound the SVK could call for a new sample aircraft from the current production batch.

In the specification data compiled for the four main seaplane types given, the 'type' aircraft that produced the largest number of series machines has been used. The main differences in the series production involved have also been noted.

CAMOUFLAGE AND MARKINGS

Initially seaplanes were not camouflage painted, their natural fabric-covered surfaces being clear doped and varnished; metal parts were finished in grey paint to resist salt water corrosion. However, from April 1917 all top surfaces were to be painted in three colours in hexagonal figures in grey-blue, grey-brown and grey-violet. All side surfaces not visible from above were to be painted grey-blue and the undersurfaces of fuselages and floats painted light-grey; the undersurface wing covering remained in natural fabric clear doped finish. Later a printed fabric with a regular hexagon pattern (the top surface colours already mentioned were dyed into the fabric) appeared, and was in widespread use on all top surfaces by the end of the war.

Usually reconnaissance seaplanes did not carry any special markings other than the national insignia in the normal locations and the large Marine aircraft number, which was approximately half the fuselage depth in height; this provided a sufficiently clear means of individual identification. However, seaplanes of the Brandenburg types operating in fighting formations from the naval air stations at Norderney, Borkum, Zeebrugge and Ostend adopted forms of markings that identified their home bases; these were white fuselage bands of various configurations on the rear fuselage immediately ahead of the tail unit and were in use at Borkum and Norderney.

At Ostend and Zeebrugge – and also at Borkum – crews embellished their machines with personal emblems that varied from heraldic coats of arms to initials and geometric symbols. These were almost always of such small size and poor legibility that they were not essential for recognition purposes, being more a form of decoration similar to that which had come into use on land-based aircraft, mostly of the fighter types.

MARINE DESIGNATION

Seaplanes of the two-seat type armed with a movable machine-gun on a rotatable gun-ring at the observer's cockpit were known as 'C class' machines. This basic designation could have suffixes added to indicate the equipment fitted – e.g., MG = additional machine-gun, FT = W/T transmitter only, and HFT = W/T transmitter and receiver. Thus C2MGFT denoted an aircraft fitted with one movable machine-gun and one fixed machine-gun (for the pilot) and equipped with a W/T transmitter; while C3MG indicated an aircraft without wireless but fitted with two fixed guns for the pilot in addition to the one movable observer's gun.

BRANDENBURG W29

Description:	Two-seat twin-float monoplane fighter
Manufacturer:	Hansa und Brandenburgische Flugzeugwerke A.G.
Marine Designation:	C3MG
Marine Number:	2204 (ordered 17/1/18, delivered 4/4/18, accepted 5/4/18)
Engine:	150hp six-cylinder water-cooled Benz (effective power 152.5hp)
Propeller:	Axial, diameter 2.75m, 1.80m pitch
Wingspan	13.5m
Length	9.35m
Height	3.1m
Weights:	
Empty	1,000kg
Loaded	1,463kg
Duration:	4 hours
Speeds:	
Take-off	98km/hr
Climb	118km/hr
Cruise	168km/hr
Rate of climb:	5.9min to 1,000m
	10.4min to 1,500m
	15.8min to 2,000m

*The normal seaworthiness rating granted to seaplanes was Condition 3 in the German sea-state table (*Seegang*) which related wind velocity to wave length, amplitude and frequency. At that time there were no means of accurately measuring the value other than estimation. (*Seegang* 3 equated to Beaufort Scale 4 (wind speed 23–27km/hr) with waves up to 2 metres high and 50 metres long.)

However, an unrestricted seaworthiness rating could be given if the seaplane successfully completed the required tests in wind velocities equating to Beaufort Scale 6 (36–44km/hr).

In the period up to 1 July 1918, 80 aircraft of this type had been ordered in the following production batches:

Marine

Number	Designation	Engine	Ordered
2201–2206	C3MG	150hp Benz	December 1917
2287–2300	C2MGHFT	150hp Benz	April 1918
2501–2506	C2MGHFT	150hp Benz	April 1918
2507–2536	C3MG	150hp Benz	April 1918
2564–2583	C2MGHFT	150hp Benz	May 1918
2584–2587	C3MG	185hp Benz	June 1918
2588–2589	C2MGHFT	185hp Benz	June 1918

BRANDENBURG W12

Description:	Two-seat twin-float biplane fighter
Manufacturer:	Hansa und Brandenburgische Flugzeugwerke A.G.
Marine Designation:	C2MG
Marine Number:	2001 (ordered 10/9/17, delivered 30/11/17, accepted 6/12/17)
Engine:	150hp six-cylinder water-cooled Benz (effective power 160hp)
Propeller:	Dr Rathjen, diameter 2.80m, pitch 1.70m
Wingspan	11.2m
Length	9.6m
Height	3.3m
Weights:	
Empty	997kg
Loaded	1,454kg
Duration:	4½ hours
Speeds:	
Take-off	90km/hr
Climb	123km/hr
Cruise	159.5km/hr
Rate of climb:	7min to 1,000m
	12min to 1,500m
	18.4min to 2,000m

In the period up to 1 July 1918, 146 aircraft of the type had been ordered in the following production batches:

Marine

Number	Designation	Engine	Ordered
1011–1016	C2MG	160hp Mercedes	October 1916
1178–1187	C2MG	150hp Benz	January 1917
1395–1414	C2MG	150hp Benz	March 1917
2000–2119	C2MG	150hp Benz	September 1917
2023–2052	C3MG	150hp Benz	October 1917
2093–2132	C2MG	160hp Mercedes	October 1917
2217–2236	C2MGHFT	160hp Mercedes	November 1917

FRIEDRICHSHAFEN FF33L

Description:	Two-seat twin-float reconnaissance biplane
Manufacturer:	Flugzeugbau Friedrichshafen GmbH
Marine Designation:	CHFT
Marine Number:	1004 (ordered 13/10/16, delivered 6/3/17, accepted 28/3/17)
Engine:	150hp six-cylinder water-cooled Benz (effective power 163hp)
Propeller:	Niendorf, diameter 2.70m, pitch 1.68m
Wingspan	13.2m
Length	8.95m
Height	4.0m
Weights:	
Empty	917kg
Loaded	1,388kg
Duration:	4 hours
Speeds:	
Take-off	81km/hr
Climb	110km/hr
Cruise	139km/hr
Rate of climb:	8min to 1,000m
	13min to 1,500m
	23.5min to 2,000m

In the period up to 1 July 1918, 135 aircraft of the type had been ordered in the following production batches:

Marine

Number	Designation	Engine	Ordered
932–941	C2MG	150hp Benz	September 1916
1001–1010	CHFT	150hp Benz	November 1916
1085–1094	CHFT	150hp Benz	October 1916
1117–1126	C2MG	150hp Benz	December 1916
1158–1177	CHFT	150hp Benz	January 1917
1234–1278	CHFT	150hp Benz	February 1917
1279–1288	C2MG	150hp Benz	February 1917
1577–1596	C2MG	150hp Benz	June 1917

FRIEDRICHSHAFEN FF49C

Description:	Two-seat twin-float reconnaissance biplane
Manufacturer:	Flugzeugbau Friedrichshafen GmbH
Marine Designation:	CHFT
Marine Number:	1699 (ordered 27/8/17, delivered 20/9/17, accepted 19/12/17)
Engine:	200hp six-cylinder water-cooled Benz (effective power 229hp)
Propeller:	Niendorf, diameter 2.96m, pitch 1.72m
Wingspan	17.8m
Length	11.65m
Height	4.45m
Weights:	
Empty	1,515kg
Loaded	2,147kg
Duration:	5¾ hours
Speeds:	
Take-off	83km/hr
Climb	118km/hr
Cruise	139.5km/hr
Rate of climb:	6.2min to 800m
	8.0min to 1,000m
	13.2min to 1,500m

In the period up to 1 July 1918, 135 aircraft of the type had been ordered in the following production batches:

Marine

Number	Designation	Engine	Ordered
1521–1535	CHFT	200hp Benz	May 1917
1597–1606	CHFT	200hp Benz	June 1917
1669–1698	CHFT	200hp Benz	July 1917
1699–1718	CHFT	200hp Benz	August 1917
1742–1811	CHFT	200hp Benz	August 1917
1812–1841	C2MGHFT	200hp Benz	August 1917
2053–2092	CHFT	200hp Benz	September 1917

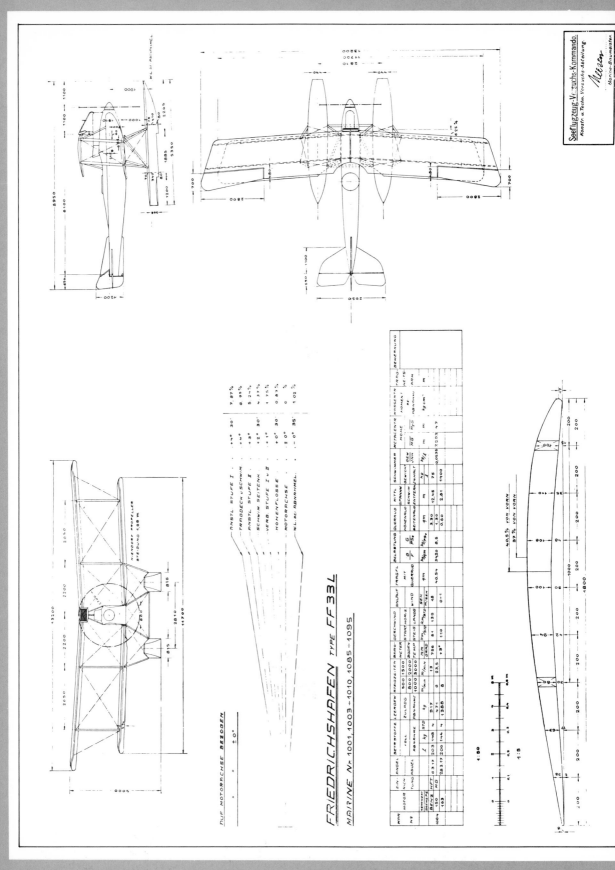

FRIEDRICHSHAFEN TYPE FF 33L

MARINE Nr. 1001, 1003 - 1010, 1085 - 1095

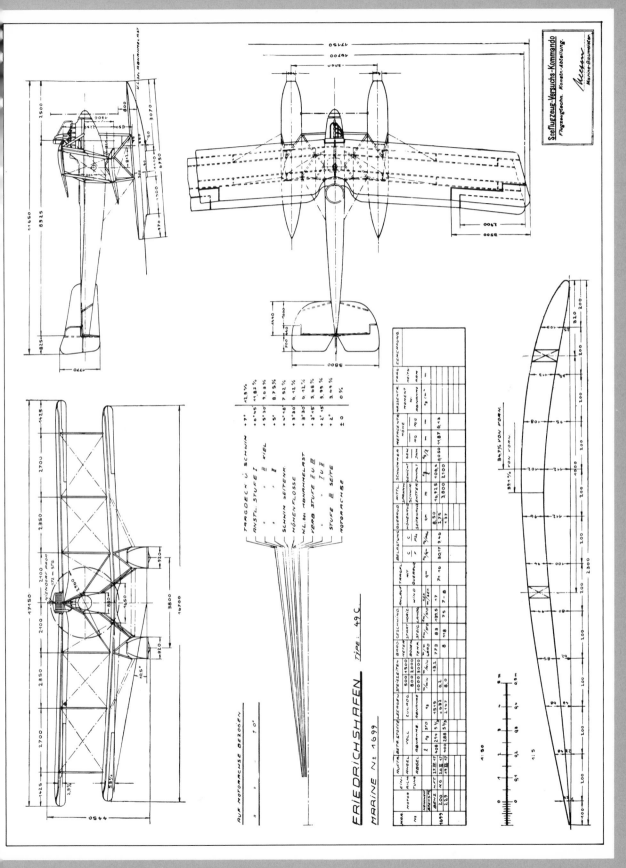

FRIEDRICHSHAFEN *Type: 49 c*

MARINE N° 1699

▲41

41. Fokker E III LF199 of *I Marine-Feldflieger-Abteilung* gets away in a cloud of castor oil smoke. In mid-September 1916 there were some 40 single-seat land fighters on naval charge, most of them Fokker E monoplanes. While a number of these were concentrated at *II Marine-Feldflieger-Abteilung* at Neumunster as a *Kampf-*

▼42

Einsitzer-Kommando, at least half of the fighter strength was deployed in the *Luftschiff-Hallenschutz-Staffeln* (Airship Shed Defence Units) at Nordholz, Tondern and other airship bases.

42. Only a few days after its acceptance on 23 September 1916, this Brandenburg KDW (748), flown by *Leutnant*

Hammer from the Baltic air station at Angernsee, forced a large four-engined Russian Sikorsky to land by repeated attacks. Despite this initial success the KDW was unpopular with its pilots; it was said to be heavy and difficult to fly, and had such a poor forward view that it was considered unsuitable for air fighting due

to the constant risk of collision that this imposed. It was known as the 'Spider' in service, due to the unusual star-strut arrangement of its interplane bracing struts. A total of 58 machines of the type was delivered, latterly having a 160hp Maybach engine in place of the 150hp Benz installed in the first production machines.

43. Personnel of the naval aviation units in Flanders were proud of their privileged location where accommodation was often in requistioned seafront hotels. Not many front-line units could boast of having private bathing beaches, but the ownership of this one, flanked by two NCO aircrew members, is clear for all to see. Although the adult civilian population was prevented by written orders from using the sand, barbed wire and military authority did not prevent many of the local children availing themselves of this facility.

44. Nine Freidrichshafen FF33 about to leave the ramp at Libau on 12 September 1916 to join with aircraft from Windau and Angernsee for a combined operation of some 20 seaplanes against Russian naval forces in the Gulf of Riga. This action saw the first operational use of twin-engined torpedo-carrying seaplanes, but their primary target, the battleship *Slava*, was not hit. The ship on the left in this picture is the seaplane-carrier SMS *Glyndwr*.

45. Sablatnig SF2 two-seat reconnaissance seaplanes about to leave the Angernsee naval air station, late 1916. Like most seaplanes used for this purpose during the first two years of the war, they carried no defensive armament. The observer occupied the front cockpit and the windmill generator for his W/T equipment can be seen at this location. Machines were operated in pairs so that one could assist the other in the event of engine or any trouble that necessitated a forced landing at sea.

43▲   44▼

45▼

▲46   ▼47

46. Naval airship L16 in flight. This Zeppelin first flew on 23 September 1915 and took part in many raids on Britain under various commanders. When the sea froze during the severe winter of 1916, L16 was used to ferry provisions to the German islands. Later used as an advanced training ship, she had carried out 235 flights when, following a forced landing at Brunsbüttel on 19 October 1917, the ship was damaged beyond repair.

47. Earlier we left RML1 in a Russian forest. . . . The machine was completely rebuilt and was modified to take an additional two engines. At this time a transparent Cellon covering to reduce the effect of searchlight illumination was under consideration and the fuselage and tail unit were covered with this material. On the first test flight on 10 March 1917, at Staaken aerodrome near Berlin, engine failure resulted in an asymmetric flight condition,

which was compounded by a control system malfunction. The pilots could not prevent the machine from crashing into the corner of one of the airship sheds.

48. *Flugmaat* Franz Wangemann of the *Marinefeldjagdstaffel* with his Albatros D III, D2288/16, at Aertrycke aerodrome in April 1917. This unit, under *Leutnant zur See* Sachsenberg, operated with success in the area of the Fourth German Army occupied by the Marine Corps. As aerial fighting activity increased, the *Staffel* was joined by other naval landplane fighter units until, towards the end of 1918, the five *Marinefeldjagdstaffeln* were formed into the *Marinefeldjagdgeschwader* under Sachsenberg. It had a strength of over 50 fighters.

49 & 50. Oskar Ursinus (Editor of *Flugsport* magazine) designed a single-seater to embrace several features intended to obtain the very best performance from the 150hp Benz six-cylinder engine. Built by Flugmaschinen Rex GmbH and allocated naval number 782, the aircraft is shown at Warnemünde during evaluation in April 1917. The most revolutionary feature of the design was its retractable float undercarriage. The pilot manually operated a small differential winch which reduced the lengths of the bracing cables on one diagonal of the undercarriage struts and lengthened corresponding cables on the other diagonal, allowing the floats to be cranked to the 'up' position. They were retracted forward against the airflow; this kept the centre of gravity forward and also assisted with float extension. In the event, the aircraft was never flown, since during initial taxiing trials at 900rpm the machine nosed over. After further investigation the design was abandoned.

48▲   49▼

50▼

▲51 ▼52

NOORD HINDER

▼53

51. Albatros W5 845 dropping a practice torpedo. Three torpedo *Staffeln* worked up in a *Sonderkommando* (Special Command) at Flensburg from mid-1916, but their operational success on both East and West Fronts was not great due to the poor performance and seaworthiness of the underpowered twin-engined seaplanes used for this duty. Various manufacturers produced torpedo seaplanes, but all were of neccessity lightly built and were demanding to fly. Eventually this weapon was discarded and the aircraft were used for other work such as mine-laying or, when fitted with extra fuel tanks, for long-range oversea reconnaissance.

52. The Dutch lightship *North Hinder* was stationed equidistant from Harwich, Hook of Holland and Zeebrugge and its locality was frequented by German submarines proceeding from the Heligoland Bight to the Channel. A British patrol area, octagonal in shape, was set up with the North Hinder as its central point – it was known as the 'Spider Web' – and provided good submarine hunting for large flying-boats based at Harwich and Felixstowe. They in their turn were harassed by the German fighting seaplanes, especially those from Zeebrugge. The ship was removed by the Dutch authorities early in 1918.

53. *Ehrenpokal 'Dem Sieger im Luftkampf'* (Victor in Air Combat). German industrialists sponsored the award of prizes of honour for an aircrew member's first aerial victory. Using the same motive and title as the Army Air Service's *Ehrenbecher*, the Navy awarded its flying personnel this handsome trophy; it could also be given for some meritorious act other than an aerial victory. The example shown, awarded to *Leutnant zur See* Eisenlohr on 22 March 1918, was for sinking the Russian destroyer *Stroiny* by bombing off the island of Oesel in the Gulf of Riga on 22 August 1917.

54. Large calibre bombs were not used against ship targets; from the beginning the principle of dropping a stick of at least five bombs straddling a target was maintained. Experience with the bombsights then in use showed that this was the correct approach. Torpedo-carrying aircraft could carry eight 58kg bombs, and it was the fifth bomb of an eight-bomb stick that sunk the Russian destroyer *Stroiny* (see previous caption). A Gotha WD 14 bomb load of approximately 300kg is shown here, made up of 10kg bombs, a size commonly used on seaplanes.

54 ▲

They are retained by a simple carrying strap across the tail of the bombs, no specially designed bomb cradles being required.

55. Torpedo-mine loaded in the torpedo crutch of a Brandenburg GW twin-engined torpedo seaplane. This weapon contained 95kg of high explosive and had to be laid from the usual torpedo dropping height of 6–8 metres (20–25ft) to prevent damage to the mine's mechanism. To gauge this height accurately at night, a weighted line was extended in a similar manner to a trailing wireless aerial. When the weight touched the surface, the drag of the water operated contacts that illuminated a light in the pilot's cockpit, indicating that the height was right for release.

55 ▼

▲ 56

56. *Santa Elena* was the seaplane-carrier with the best performance; she had a displacement of 7,415brt and could carry four seaplanes in her hangars and another four

▼ 57

on deck. During the operation against the Russian-held island of Oesel in September 1917, this ship was used to advantage and was a floating base for 16 seaplanes, which were moored

to a boom and buoys when the ship was at anchor. The slow speed of the seaplane-carriers (only 10 knots in the case of *Santa Elena*) did not allow the use of such vessels in

conjunction with other naval forces. Their main value was as mobile advanced naval air stations.

57. Zeebrugge was the largest and most active of the Flanders coastal air stations and the number of aircraft operated by the different units based there sometimes exceeded 50 seaplanes, although the normal establishment was 35 aircraft. Seen here is a train-load of Friedrichshafen FF33s in late 1917, a type that gave excellent service but which was then being replaced by the higher-performance Brandenburg W12.

58. Christiansen flying one of the early production Brandenburg W12 seaplanes powered by a 150hp Benz engine. This aircraft, 1183, served at Zeebrugge for eight months before it was destroyed in a bombing attack on the Mole on 10 May 1918. Designed by Ernst Heinkel late in 1916, the W12's performance was equal to that of the single-seat seaplanes then in service. Capable of 160km/hr (100mph), its rate of climb and general manoeuvrability made it popular with the crews, who gave it the name 'Kamel'.

59. Carrier-pigeons formed an important part of the equipment of seaplanes. The birds were released with position information if a machine was forced to land on the water, and many crews and aircraft were saved as a result. While Brandenburg W12 1399 at Zeebrugge is bombed-up prior to flight, pigeons are checked into their special wicker basket for stowing on board.

60. Since seaplane engines could not be run up to test their power output and serviceability immediately before flight when on the water, this was done either on the ramp before launching or, as shown here, with a Zeebrugge Friedrichshafen FF49C, before lifting the aircraft by crane for lowering to the water. To the rear of the floats can be seen the flat railway car used to move the seaplane from its hangar to the crane.

58 ▲   59 ▼

60 ▼

▲61   ▼62   ▼63

61. Having an increased length of 743ft and a volume of 2,418,700cu ft, Zeppelin L59 under the command of *Kapitänleutnant* Bockholt left Jamboli in Bulgaria on 21 November 1917 with 15 tons of ammunition and medical supplies for forces in German East Africa. Near Khartoum the ship was recalled due to the hopelessness of General von Lettow-Vorbeck's position. When she landed back at Jamboli on 25 November after 95 hours in the air, having covered some 4,200 miles, sufficient fuel for a further 64 hours' flight remained in her tanks.

64 ▲

62. British non-rigid coastal airship C-27 falling in flames into the sea off Lowestoft on 11 December 1917 after being attacked by a three-strong Brandenburg W12 fighting reconnaissance formation led by *Oberleutnant* Christiansen. On that day the triangular patrol route usually taken from Zeebrugge, which resulted in a sweep up the British coast, was carried out in reverse, and it was at the northernmost turning point for a run down the coast that the Pulham-based C-27 was first seen. During this action a series of photographs was taken with a hand-held 25cm camera by *Leutnant* Ehrhardt, the observer on *Flug-Ober-Maat* Urban's aircraft.

63. Friedrich Christiansen came from a seafaring family, had already served some years in the merchant service, and held his Master's certificate before he learned to fly in 1914 at the age of 34. By the outbreak of war he was an experienced pilot and quickly converted to seaplanes and was sent to Zeebrugge in January 1915. Commissioned early in 1916, he rose to become Station Commander in September 1917 and by the end of the war held the rank of *Kapitänleutnant*. Christiansen was responsible for the ever-

improving standard of the work done from the Flanders coastal stations; he personally devised many of the fighting tactics used, and he knew the North Sea area like no other.

64. When SMS *Wolf* left Kiel on 30 November 1916 on a 15-month voyage, during which she traversed three oceans as a commerce raider, she carried a Friedrichshafen FF33E seaplane on board for scouting purposes. Named 'Wölfchen', the seaplane played an important part in *Wolf*'s marauding activities and carried out over 50 flights in this role. This photograph, taken on 6 March 1918, shows the aircraft redecorated after its triumphant return; during the voyage 'Wölfchen' was operated without the display of any national insignia other than the German War Ensign, which was flown from the innermost starboard rear interplane strut as occasion demanded.

65. Crew of 'Wölfchen', *Leutnant zur See* Stein (left) and *Oberflugmeister* Fabeck pose in front of their seaplane on 6 March 1918 after their long voyage, during which *Wolf* sank, mined or captured 28 Allied vessels, and returned home loaded with booty from her victims. For much of the

time the aircraft was exposed on deck to tropical heat and heavy rain; extensive renovation was necessary to her fabric-covered surfaces, the mainplanes

eventually being re-covered in heavyweight silk overpainted with grey oil paint.

65 ▼

▲66

66. This R-Class flying-boat, 1431 was the only four-engined monoplane to see active duty with the Navy. Seen at Norderney after its delivery flight from Zeppelin-Werke Lindau at Seemos on Lake Constance on 19 February 1918, it was intended for long-range oversea reconnaissance but was not officially cleared for front-line use until 27 October 1918. A number of flights of over 10 hours' duration had been made by the time of the Armistice, and the machine served on mine-clearing operations after the war until broken up on Allied orders at the end of July 1921.

▼67

67. Three examples of the Brandenburg W20 single-seat flying-boat were built, the so-called 'type' aircraft which was the example of any new design evaluated by the seaplane experimental centre (SVK) at Warnemünde before being accepted for naval use (by the SAK). 1552 is seen on 14 March 1918. Intended to be carried as an aerial scout on submarines, it did not see operational service. The W20 was designed to be assembled and dismantled very quickly, using the minimum of hand tools; individual components were stowed in watertight air tubes on the submarine's deck.

68. Brandenburg W19 from Norderney showing the white chevron unit marking on the rear fuselage. This aircraft was an enlarged, more powerful version of the W12 with an extended radius of action, but before it reached the front in any numbers it, in its turn, had been outdated by the Brandenburg W29 monoplane.

69. Friedrichshafen FF41A twin-engined torpedo seaplane 997 entering the water; the wheeled chassis under the floats being restrained through ropes by the handling crew. When in deep enough water the buoyancy of the floats lifted the aircraft from the wheeled chassis, which was then retrieved and usually stowed on the slipway for a reverse operation when the seaplane returned.

70. Beaching party, suitably attired in waterproof suits, bringing in Friedrichshafen FF49C 1778. When beaching did not allow seaplanes to run up the slipway to have the wheeled chassis fitted, the aircraft was stopped a few yards from the shore and the aircrew were taken off pick-a-back style; the handling crew then walked the machine on to the wheeled chassis and pulled the aircraft up the ramp out of the water.

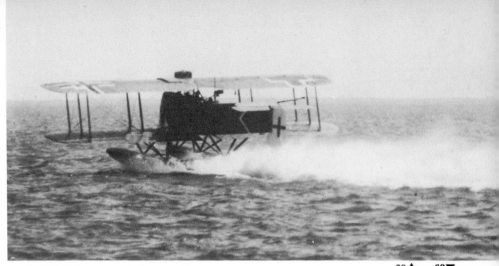

68▲ 69▼

70▼

▲71

71. Friedrichshafen FF49C from Norderney investigating a suspicious sailing ship. Vessels stopped in prohibited areas and found to have contraband goods aboard were either directed to a German port or destroyed. Initially airships were used for this surveillance, since they could provide crew members to take over shipboard duties, but the risk to the large hydrogen-filled airships was quickly deemed to be too great and this duty was performed by seaplanes for most of the war.

▼72

72. Engine change at Aertrycke. The reliability of aero-engines increased steadily as the war progressed and by 1918 the 165hp Mercedes six-cylinder water-cooled engine was relatively trouble-free. Such mechanical failings as did appear were usually rectified without having to take the engine out of the airframe. A serious problem is indicated here; even the wing radiator has been removed. While the replacement engine for this Albatros D Va of *I Marinefeldjagdstaffel* hangs on the block and tackle of the sheer-legs, the unserviceable motor on its temporary transport (which uses aeroplane wheels) is at the right, beside the cradle for moving the engine to the overhaul shop.

73. Christiansen in Brandenburg W29 2512 (left) over the naval air station at Kiel-Holtenau en route to Zeebrugge. As soon as aircraft of this type had passed their acceptance trials, Christiansen journeyed to Warnemünde with his crews and flew the machines to Zeebrugge. The first five seaplanes collected in this manner landed at Zeebrugge on 1 July 1918 and were used operationally the following morning.

74. Close-up of the nose of a Brandenburg W29 showing details of radiator, cowling and the forward-firing LMG 08 with its ammunition chute. The instability of phosphorus cartridges caused the weapons section of the SVK to investigate the internal ammunition stowages on forward-firing seaplane guns. It was found that the W29 installation raised the temperature of the ammunition by 15°C due to the proximity of the engine mass. At outside air temperatures of 25°C the final temperature was sufficiently below the 50° danger point that induced spontaneous combustion of the unreliable cartridges, and the W29 was given a clean bill of health.

75. On 6 July 1918 Christiansen's *IC Staffel* flying five W29 monoplanes caught the British submarine *C-25* on the surface off the British coast and immediately attacked it. During the action some 5,000 machine-gun rounds were fired at the boat and it was sufficiently disabled to prevent its being able to submerge. By now out of ammunition, the W29s were forced to return to Zeebrugge. During this action *Leutnant* Ehrhardt was able to secure some remarkable photographs; this one taken over the pilot's shoulder shows the low altitude used on the seaplanes's firing passes.

76. Three Brandenburg W29s of Christiansen's *IC Staffel* landing back at Zeebrugge. The Mole, a mile-long 80yd-wide curved breakwater of solid concrete, jutted out into the sea and afforded the necessary protection to the twin piers

▲75

(seen in the background) that guarded the entrance to the inner basins and the Bruges Canal. Seaplane operations took place in this sheltered area, and regardless of the state of the outer sea, it was unusual if seaplanes could not operate when required.

77. British Felixstowe F.2A twin-engined flying-boat 4305 from Great Yarmouth burning on the water off Lowestoft on 31 July 1918, yet another victim of the speedy Brandenburg W29 and the aggressiveness of Christiansen's *IC Staffel*. Once again *Leutnant* Ehrhardt

secured photographs of the action, and his series of six pictures showed that the boat had been hit and set on fire in the air during the first attack by the five-strong W29 formation. Previous encounters with these boats by the slower Brandenburg W12 had not

▼76

77▲

78▲

always been successful, but the extra speed of the new monoplane meant that closure to effective firing range was now assured.

78. Late model of the twin-screw remote-controlled missile boat that formed the equipment of *Fernlenkzuge I* and *II* based at Ostend and Blankenberghe. The boats had explosive warheads of up to 500kg and were propelled at over 30 knots towards their targets by 240hp 8-cylinder diesel engines. Steering instructions were via a multi-strand cable which could be as long as 35 kilometres (20 miles). The land-based controller received his information from the observer of a Friedrichshafen FF49C seaplane using direct push-button wireless control. The low success rate of these boats was attributed to the shortcomings of the cable control system. By November 1918, however, a method of direct wireless guidance from the aircraft to the boat had been devised and would have been in operational use by February 1919 had the war continued.

79. Another form of cable-controlled missile – Siemens torpedo glider under the hull of Zeppelin L35. Although this weapon did not reach operational status, the improved system for the missile boats might have resurrected the torpedo glider. It was not flown into the target (but it could have been). At a suitable position and height, a special signal caused the airframe components to detach from the torpedo, which then entered the water and continued towards its ship target in the usual manner.

79▼

▲80 ▼81

Frega
St

▼82

80. Not only did two-seat high-performance landplanes like this Halberstadt CL II serve in the two *Marine Schlachtstaffeln* on ground support work with the naval infantry, and on oversea air-fighting duties as required, but a number were also used at night by a special naval unit (*Masosta*) under *Leutnant* Majewski against the frequent penetrations of Handley Pages bombing the U-boat installations at Bruges.

81. *Fregattenkapitän* Peter Strasser was the Commander of the Naval Airship Division from October 1913 until 23 November 1916 when he was given overall command with the creation of the new title, Leader of Airships (*Führer der Luftschiffe* – FdL). The remarkable achievements of this force were directly due to his outstanding drive and ability. Devoted to his ships and men, he never lost faith in the airship as a weapon, despite the severe losses encountered. He was awarded the *Ordre Pour le Mérite* on 20 August 1917 and was killed with the rest of the crew of L70 (*Kapitänleutnant* von Lossnitzer) when it was shot down in flames off the Norfolk coast on 3 August 1918 in the last airship raid of the war against the United Kingdom.

82. The approach of the Royal Navy's Harwich Light Cruiser Force into the Heligoland Bight on 11 August 1918 was reported by routine seaplane reconnaissance and a hot reception awaited the six coastal motor boats carried by the cruisers and launched at the edge of the German minefield to operate inshore. Borkum and Norderney seaplane stations despatched fighting aircraft and in the resulting action all the CMBs were lost. The first CMB to be put out of action was hit in the engine and in the smoke-screen chemical tank. Its neighbour's wake can be seen as it circles back to the stricken boat to take off the crew. It was the combined Lewis gun fire from these two boats that brought down the only German seaplane lost, 2297, a Brandenburg W29 from Norderney, whose crew (*Flugmaat* Nagorsnick and *Flugzeug Matrose* Wohlfeil) were killed.

83. Zeppelin L53 being walked into Factory Shed 1 at Friedrichshafen. Commissioned on 21 August 1917, this airship made some 50 flights under the command of *Kapitänleutnant* Prölss and was the last Zeppelin to be lost in the war. During the

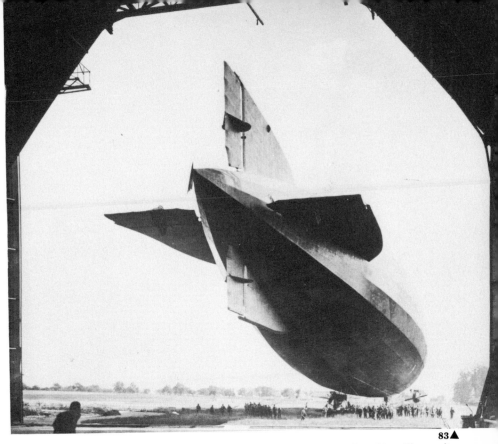

83▲

same operation that involved the loss of six Royal Navy coastal motor boats off Terschelling, L53 was shot down in flames by Lieutenant S. D. Culley in a Sopwith Camel which had accompanied the Harwich Force; he took off from a destroyer-towed lighter and at the end of his sortie ditched in the sea, after which both he and

his Camel were recovered.

84. Fighting seaplanes operated alone initially, but the emergence of Allied formations over the sea and the example provided by the fighter formation work in the German Army Air Service led to the establishment of the 'C-Staffeln' which operated in strengths of

3, 5 or 7 machines. These units did not confine themselves to pure aerial fighting but undertook reconnaissance work in all its forms. This is a *C-Staffel* of five Brandenburg W29 monoplanes from Borkum, identified by the white oblique band carried on the fuselage ahead of the tail unit.

84▼

▲85

85. This Rumpler C VII, C8179/17, was on the strength of the *Seefrontstaffel (Seefrosta)*. Flown by *Leutnants* Voigt and Rowehl, it carried out many long-range reconnaissance flights, some of over three hours' duration, extending to the English coast, into the Thames Estuary and the Channel. Undertaken in conditions of good visibility, such forays gathered much information concerning shipping movements, especially activities on the coastal explosive mine net barrages that protected the safe lanes used by Allied shipping.

86. *Kapitänleutnant* Freiherr Treusch von Buttlar-Brandenfels served throughout

▼87

▲86